KEEPING PETS

Rabbits

Louise and Richard Spilsbury

Heinemann
LIBRARY

www.heinemann.co.uk/library
Visit our website to find out more information about Heinemann Library books.

To order:
☎ Phone 44 (0) 1865 888066
📄 Send a fax to 44 (0) 1865 314091
💻 Visit the Heinemann bookshop at www.heinemann.co.uk/library to browse
our catalogue and order online.

First published in Great Britain by
Heinemann Library, Halley Court, Jordan Hill,
Oxford OX2 8EJ, part of Harcourt Education.

Heinemann is a registered trademark of
Harcourt Education Ltd.

Editorial: Andrew Farrow and Stig Vatland
Design: Richard Parker and Q2A Solutions
Picture Research: Maria Joannou and
Virginia Stroud-Lewis
Production: Chloe Bloom

Originated by Modern Age Repro
Printed and Bound in China
by South China Printing Company

10 digit ISBN: 0 431 12449 3
13 digit ISBN: 978 0 431 12449 0

10 09 08 07 06
10 9 8 7 6 5 4 3 2 1

**British Library Cataloguing in Publication
Data**
Spilsbury, Louise and Richard, 1956-
Rabbits.
- (Keeping pets)
636.9'322
A full catalogue record for this book is available
from the British Library.

Acknowledgements
The publishers would like to thank the following
for permission to reproduce photographs: Alamy
Images p. **7 top**; Ardea p. **9 bottom**; Ardea
(John Daniels) pp. **8, 9 top, 12, 13**; Brian
Warling pp. **21 top, 22 top**; Malcolm Harris p.
17 top; NHPA pp. **4, 7 bottom**; RSPCA
Photolibrary p. **9 middle**; Harcourt Education
Ltd (Tudor Photography) pp. **5, 6, 10, 11, 14, 15,
16, 17 bottom, 18, 19 bottom, 19 top, 21
bottom, 22 bottom, 22 top, 23, 24 bottom,
24 top, 25 bottom, 25 top, 26, 27 left, 27
right, 28, 29 bottom, 29 top, 30 bottom, 30
top, 31, 32, 33 bottom, 33 top, 34, 35
bottom, 35 top, 36 bottom, 36 top, 37, 38
bottom, 38 top, 39, 40 bottom, 40 top, 41, 42
bottom, 42 top, 43, 44 bottom, 44 top, 45**.

Cover photograph reproduced with permission of
Harcourt Education Limited (Tudor photography).

Every effort has been made to contact copyright
holders of any material reproduced in this book.
Any omissions will be rectified in subsequent
printings if notice is given to the publishers.

The paper used to print this book comes from
sustainable resources.

Contents

Any words appearing in the text in bold, **like this**, are explained in the Glossary.

What is a rabbit?

Rabbits make delightful pets. Rabbits are clever, lively, and interested in the world around them. When they are treated well, they can be friendly and loving companions.

Around the world, wild rabbits are considered **pests** because they eat farmers' crops. Some pet rabbits look a bit like wild rabbits, but they are quite different. Pet rabbits are European wild rabbits that have been tamed or **domesticated**.

Wild rabbits live together in large groups. Sometimes hundreds of rabbits live together in one area.

History of pet rabbits

There have been wild rabbits on Earth for millions of years. Around 1,000 years ago, people began to keep rabbits in pens. They used the rabbits for food and fur. Around 500 years ago, monks successfully tamed rabbits. By the 20th century, people were keeping rabbits as pets.

A pet rabbit will need you to feed and care for it for the whole of its life.

Famous rabbits

There are many famous rabbits, such as the Easter bunny, the white rabbit in *Alice's Adventures in Wonderland*, and Bugs Bunny. Can you think of any more?

Need to know

- Children cannot buy their own pet rabbits. You must take an adult with you when you go to choose a rabbit.
- In many countries there are laws that protect pets such as rabbits. If you have a pet, you have to make sure it is well cared for. For example, that means giving it enough food and water, and keeping it clean, healthy, and safe.

Rabbit facts

Rabbits are a kind of **mammal**. Mammals are animals that have some hair or fur on their bodies and are **warm-blooded**. That means they can warm up or cool down to keep their body at a steady temperature. Mammals also feed their young on milk from their own body.

Eyes, ears, and noses

Rabbits are most lively in the morning and early evening, and they often nap during the day. Rabbits have large eyes to help them see all around, and they have excellent senses of hearing and smell. Most rabbits have long ears that stand up and can twist in the direction of a sound. The rabbit's twitching nose gives it a much better sense of smell than any human has.

Rabbit whiskers are as long as a rabbit is wide. Rabbits use their whiskers to tell if a space is wide enough for them to get through.

Did you know?

- Rabbits live from five to ten years.
- Male rabbits are called bucks.
- Female rabbits are called does.
- Baby rabbits are called kittens.
- Adult rabbits grow to about 40 centimetres (16 inches) long.
- Male rabbits are usually slightly bigger and heavier than female rabbits.
- Rabbits have sharp front teeth that keep growing throughout their lives.

Rabbit babies

Adult female rabbits can have several **litters** of kittens a year. There are between three and nine baby rabbits in each litter. Kittens are born with their eyes closed and they cannot see. For the first ten days, they cannot hear, and they have no hair.

Rabbit life

In the wild, rabbits live together in large groups. One of the things that makes a rabbit such a good pet is that they are animals that need and like company. In the wild, rabbits sleep in **burrows** in the ground that they dig out with their front feet. You may find that your pet rabbit likes to dig, too!

Rabbits keep their teeth the right length by chewing things.

Baby rabbits are completely helpless and depend on their mother to feed them and care for them.

A wide choice

There are about 50 types or **breeds** of pet rabbit in the world, so there are a lot to choose from. Pet rabbits come in a variety of colours, including white, sand, speckled, patterned, grey, and black. Different breeds of rabbit also have different kinds of fur. Some kinds, like the Angora, have long fluffy fur. Others, such as the Agouti, have short, straight hair, which is brown with some black in it.

Different sizes

Rabbits also come in different sizes. Some types are small and only weigh about 2.5 kilograms (5–6 pounds) when they are adults. These include the Netherland Dwarf rabbit and the Lionhead, which has very long hair around its neck. Medium-sized rabbits include the Rex with its velvety hair, and the Angora. The largest breeds of rabbit weigh between 5 and 10 kilograms (11–22 pounds). The British giant or Giant Papillion can reach the weight of a small dog!

A Netherland dwarf rabbit.

Crossbreeds

When two different breeds of rabbit produce young, the kittens are cross-breeds, not pure-breds. They often look like a mixture of both their parents.

Big ears

Some rabbits have really long ears. They are called lop-eared rabbits. French lop-eared rabbits have big droopy ears that hang down below their jaw line. English lop-eared rabbits have ears so long that they drag on the floor!

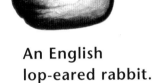

An English lop-eared rabbit.

A Lionhead rabbit.

A Giant Papillion rabbit.

Are rabbits for you?

Rabbits make great pets for people of all ages. However, before you get a pet, there are a lot of things to think about. Rabbits live a long time, so you need to think very carefully about the good and not-so-good points about having one as a pet.

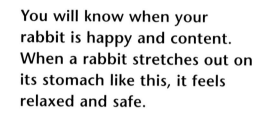

You will know when your rabbit is happy and content. When a rabbit stretches out on its stomach like this, it feels relaxed and safe.

Rabbit good points

- Most pet rabbits are gentle, cuddly, affectionate, and playful.
- Most rabbits are calm and enjoy being with people.
- Rabbits are easy to care for and cheap to feed.
- Rabbits live for five to ten years, which is longer than most small pets, such as guinea pigs.

Rabbit not-so-good points

- Rabbits need big **hutches** to live in and large **runs** to exercise in. These can be expensive and take up a lot of space.
- You should take your rabbits to the vet every year for a check-up and they may need treatment if they become ill. This can be expensive.
- Frightened rabbits can kick and scratch hard.
- If your rabbit plays indoors, it may leave droppings or **urine** (wee) on the floor that you will have to clean up.
- Male rabbits that are not **neutered** may spray urine and rub against people.

A pet rabbit can become a great friend.

Yes or no?

Before you get a rabbit you need to think carefully about these good and not-so-good points. Are you prepared to spend time each and every day with your rabbits for their whole lives? Will you feed them daily and clean out their cages regularly? If you think you can provide everything a rabbit needs, then yes, you are ready to own a rabbit!

Choosing your rabbit

Almost all types of rabbit make good pets, but some need different amounts and types of care. Think carefully before buying large types of rabbit or ones with long hair.

Choosing large breeds

A rabbit that is a very large **breed** costs much more to keep. They eat more food, they need very large **hutches** to live in, and big **runs** to exercise in. They may also need more veterinary care. Large rabbits may be too heavy for you to pick up when they are fully-grown. If they kick or bite you, it can really hurt.

Top tip

All rabbits start off small, but some may get very big. Make sure you know how big a baby rabbit will become before you buy it!

Most young people choose short-haired rabbits, like this Brown Dutch.

Choosing smaller breeds

All rabbits have their own individual personalities. The very small breeds of rabbit look cute, but they may be too nervous to get used to being with children. Most people get a medium-sized breed because they are usually happy to be handled, but they will not get too big to hold.

Choosing long-haired rabbits

Many people do not have time to look after a long-haired rabbit. If you choose one, it is very important that you prevent its hair from getting tangled or matted. This takes a lot of time and effort. You have to brush the rabbit all over for at least 20 minutes every day. You will also need to take it to the vet to have its hair clipped once in a while. Long-haired rabbits leave a lot of fluff around the house and often get **fur balls**. Fur balls are lumps of hair that get caught in the throat after rabbits have licked themselves clean.

Angora rabbits have long, silky coats of hair. It takes a lot of hard work to keep long-haired rabbits like this healthy and happy.

One or more?

Pet rabbits are much happier if you keep two or more together for company. If you get more than one, try to get them from the same family. Does (females) usually get along well, but bucks (males) may fight. Some people keep just one pet rabbit, but you have to give a single rabbit a lot of attention to keep it happy.

What if rabbits fight?

- If rabbits fight, you may have to separate them quickly before one gets hurt.
- Wear thick gloves in case the rabbits bite or scratch you.
- Keep them apart for a while. Then allow them to come together gradually until they get used to each other.
- Never leave them alone until you are sure they will not fight.

Male or female?

Both male and female rabbits make good pets. You should have them **neutered** or **spayed** by a vet when they are young, so they cannot have babies. This operation does not hurt the rabbit. There is a slight risk involved, because some rabbits may react badly to **anaesthetics**. Neutered or spayed rabbits make much more peaceful and happier pets. Neutered bucks will live happily together and will not fight. They will not spray smelly **urine**.

Two sister rabbits live very happily together.

How old?

People usually get young rabbits because they are easier to tame and handle. Baby rabbits are ready to leave their mothers at around nine weeks old. If you are getting more than one rabbit, it is much better to get young rabbits. They are more likely to live happily together.

Rabbits and guinea pigs

Some people keep guinea pigs and rabbits together, but animal care experts like the **RSPCA** do not think this is a good idea. They say it is better to keep two or more rabbits together.

This baby rabbit is nine weeks old and ready to leave her mother.

Buying from a breeder

Many people get a rabbit from a private **breeder**. Private breeders know all about the animals and usually breed strong, healthy, good-natured rabbits. Private breeders handle their young rabbits often, so they are used to being with people. When you go to a breeder's, you can also see the rabbit's parents to make sure they are healthy, and you can find out your rabbit's exact date of birth. You can find the names of local private breeders on the Internet, at the library, or by asking a vet.

Ask to stroke or look closely at a rabbit so you can tell if it is friendly and healthy.

Pet shops and rescue homes

If you buy your rabbit from a pet shop, find one where the staff know about rabbits. Check that they have kept males and females in separate **hutches**, otherwise you may end up with a pregnant rabbit. Some people get a rabbit from a **rescue home** or **animal shelter**. These are places that take in rabbits from people who are unable to look after them properly. It can be very rewarding to look after a rescued rabbit and give it a second chance of a happy life.

What to look for

When you choose a rabbit, there are several things to watch out for. Make sure the rabbits are living in a clean place. Look at all the rabbits. If just one is sick, it may mean that others are sick, too. Healthy rabbits should not be too fat or too thin. They should have smooth coats and be clean, bright-eyed, and alert.

Choose a rabbit that looks healthy and happy. It should have a clean nose and ears, bright eyes, and a shiny coat.

When you choose a rabbit, make sure the cages are clean and not overcrowded, and that the rabbits look healthy.

Top tips

- Choose a rabbit that looks lively and playful.
- Make sure your rabbit does not have runny or sticky eyes or ears, or a wet or dirty bottom.
- Check the fur to see that it is not matted or patchy, and that there are no cuts or rashes.

17

What do I need?

Before you bring your new pet rabbits home, you need to make sure you have everything they will need. The most important things they need are somewhere to live and somewhere to exercise.

Hutch

Most people keep their rabbit in a wooden **hutch**. An outdoor hutch has legs to keep it off damp ground and a sloping roof so rain runs off it. Place it somewhere out of strong wind, rain, and sun, and safe from other animals. Move the hutch to a sheltered place in cold weather.

Top tips

- Rabbits need a lot of space, so get as big a hutch as you can.
- A hutch should be at least four times the length of an adult rabbit that is lying stretched out.
- It should be high enough for a rabbit to stand on its back legs without its ears touching the roof.
- Remember, the more rabbits you have, the bigger the hutch you should get.

Rabbit hutches have two parts. One side has a solid wooden door to stop draughts and to make a private area. The other side has a wire mesh front to let in fresh air. It also lets the rabbits see out.

Flooring and bedding

Before you put your rabbit into the hutch, line the floor with newspaper and cover that with wood shavings. Then put hay or shredded paper into the sleeping side of the hutch. Your rabbit will use this to make itself a bed! Do not use straw for bedding. Straw has sharp edges that can injure a rabbit's eyes.

Newspaper and wood shavings on the hutch floor make it more comfortable for your rabbit. They also soak up **urine**.

Rabbits like to make themselves a little nest to sleep in.

Top tips

- Do not use cedar wood shavings because they can harm your rabbit.
- If you have a long-haired rabbit, do not use wood shavings on the floor. Shavings get tangled in the rabbit's fur and cause knots.

Wire and plastic cages

Some people keep their rabbits indoors. Indoor rabbits need a cage to sleep and rest in, where they can feel safe and hidden. Indoor rabbit cages usually have a deep plastic or metal base and a hard wire top. They are light-weight and easy to clean, and the bases do not soak up **urine** like wood does. Choose as large a cage as possible and add flooring just as you would for an outdoor hutch. Put hay bedding in a wooden or cardboard box for the rabbit to sleep in.

Put your rabbit's cage somewhere out of the sun, away from draughts or heaters, and out of reach of any other pets you have.

Litter trays

When your rabbits are playing in your house, you need to give them a **litter tray** to be their toilet. Most rabbits are very clean animals and you can easily train them to use a plastic litter tray.

Put the tray in a quiet spot and line it with newspaper covered with hay or pet litter. Do not use cat litter, because it is bad for rabbits.

How to litter-train rabbits

- Start in a small room for the first few days.
- Put in one or two litter trays and add a little soiled (dirty) bedding from the rabbit cage so the trays smell right.
- Rabbits produce droppings as they eat, so put hay or a food bowl at one end of the litter tray to encourage them.
- You can let your rabbit roam in the house once it is litter-trained.
- Be warned – rabbits may still make a mess on the floor sometimes!

If you keep your rabbit indoors, you will need to buy a cage with a plastic or metal bottom and hard wire top.

Top tip

If your rabbit goes to the toilet on the floor while he is still being trained, clean the area with a little vinegar. Rabbits hate the smell and will not urinate there again.

Rabbit urine can be very smelly, so change the litter in your rabbit's tray every day. Rabbits will not use litter boxes that are dirty and smelly.

21

Outdoor runs

Rabbits are lively animals that need several hours of exercise every day. Rabbits like to exercise outdoors in the fresh air. **Runs** or pens keep rabbits safe outside. You can buy one or make your own, but make sure you get a run that is large and has four sides, a roof, and a floor. The roof stops your rabbits jumping out and stops other animals from getting in. A wire mesh floor prevents them from digging their way out. Many runs have a covered end where the rabbits can hide from bad weather. If yours does not, you must put the run somewhere under shelter or fix up a cover over one end.

It is a good idea to have a covered end, where your rabbits can shelter from sun, wind, or rain.

Where to put outdoor runs

Put the run in a quiet part of the garden on healthy grass. It should be out of wind and bright sunlight, and away from other pets. Check on your rabbits regularly and always bring them indoors or back to their hutch before dark. If you move the rabbit run to a new spot every day, your rabbits will have fresh grass to eat and you will not ruin your family's lawn!

Rabbits love the chance to play in the fresh air.

Indoor exercise

When rabbits exercise indoors, it is very important to make sure they are safe. Shut doors so they cannot escape and other animals cannot get in. Cover electrical wires or tape them up out of the way. A rabbit could be burned or **electrocuted** by just one bite of a wire. Move any houseplants out of reach because rabbits may get ill if they chew them. Move or cover furniture or other items that your family does not want the rabbit to chew.

Top tips

- Make sure you close and lock the door of an outside run.
- Make sure your rabbit always has fresh water to drink, indoors or outside.

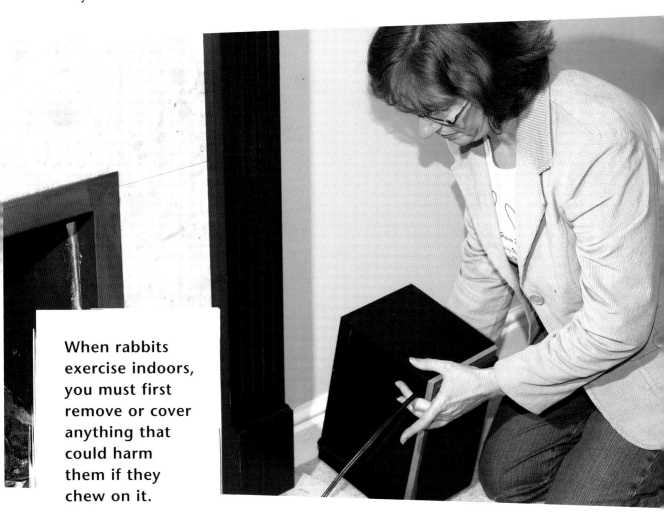

When rabbits exercise indoors, you must first remove or cover anything that could harm them if they chew on it.

Looking after your rabbit

Rabbits need your attention every day. You need to make sure that they always have fresh water, that their cage is clean, and that they are healthy. You also need to give them the right types of food.

Dried food

Most pet shops sell a variety of different dried food mixes for rabbits. These contain **grains**, pellets, and dried vegetables, such as peas. Experiment by buying small amounts of different types until you know which kind your rabbit likes best.

Your rabbit may like some types of dried food more than others.

Hay

Hay is an essential part of your rabbit's daily diet. Nibbling hay keeps his teeth and jaws strong, and provides a lot of **fibre** to keep his stomach healthy. Put the hay in a hayrack to stop him soiling it or walking on it.

Make sure you give your rabbit hay that is dry, clean, and free from dust, mould, or **parasites**. Buy rabbit hay from a pet shop or a good farm supplier.

Hay keeps your rabbit healthy.

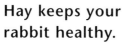

Food facts
- Small rabbits eat about a tablespoon of dried food each day.
- Large rabbits eat twice as much or more.
- If there is a lot left over, give less food the next day.
- Rabbits eat more as they get older.

Why does my rabbit eat his droppings?
Some of the food that rabbits eat goes through their **digestive system** before they have taken all the **nutrients** from it. They eat this food a second time, in the form of special soft droppings, to get more nutrients from their food.

Fresh food
Your rabbits can also eat a small amount of raw, fresh fruit or vegetables every day. Most rabbits like crunchy foods such as carrots, celery, and pears. Wash them first and cut them into pieces. To give you an idea of the right amounts to give, a small rabbit might eat a carrot and a small piece of pear each day. A large rabbit could have two celery sticks and half an apple.

Rabbits eat these soft and shiny droppings. They do not eat their waste droppings, which are hard and raisin-like.

Try giving your rabbits very small amounts of fresh food at first, until you know whether they like it.

25

Foods to avoid

Certain foods can make rabbits ill. These include dried food mixes intended for other small animals and some fresh foods, including apple seeds, raw potato, rhubarb, and tomato leaves. Many garden plants are poisonous, so if your rabbit is outside in her **run**, make sure she cannot reach and eat anything other than grass. Only give small amounts of leafy vegetables such as cabbage because these can give rabbits **diarrhoea**.

Treats

If people eat snack foods too often, they get overweight and suffer from tooth decay. It is the same for rabbits. Too many treats can also give rabbits serious stomach problems. Pet shops sell a wide range of treat foods for rabbits, but not all of them are good for your pet. Ask your vet before you buy treat foods from a pet store. Or stick to healthy treats such as broccoli, a few raisins, a strawberry, or a raspberry.

Rabbits get very excited when offered a healthy treat.

Chewing blocks

Many rabbits like to chew on mineral blocks from pet shops or the fresh bark from apple tree branches. These are good for rabbits' teeth, but avoid wood from cherry, plum, cedar, or redwood trees.

Water supply

Rabbits must always have a constant supply of clean, fresh water. Most people attach a plastic bottle to the side of the hutch. This type of bottle drips water when the rabbit puts its mouth to it. Do not forget to attach a water bottle to an outside run too – your rabbit needs water when she is exercising. Check water bottles at least once a day, especially in summer when rabbits may drink a lot of water because it is hot.

Top tip

In winter, water in bottles on outdoor hutches can freeze and that means your rabbit has nothing to drink. Solve this problem by wrapping some padding or thick cloth around the bottle and check it every day.

Water bottles with a drip-feed metal spout are best. The ones with ball-bearings in the tube leak less than those without.

Secure your rabbit's water bottle to the side of the cage at a height that she can reach easily.

Cleaning out

An important part of looking after your rabbits is keeping their hutch clean. Rabbits are tidy animals but they need some help from you. Here is a guide to tell you what to do and when to do it.

Rabbits are clean animals and they like having a clean cage.

Daily cleaning

You need to do some cleaning jobs every day. Ask an adult to help you. Remove rabbit droppings from the cage or hutch using a plastic scoop and flush them down the toilet. Remove wet bedding and any dirty flooring, and replace with clean, dry sawdust or wood shavings. Change the litter in the rabbit's **litter tray** every day. Check your rabbit's food dish. Throw away any stale, uneaten food from the dish and then wash and dry the bowl.

Cleaning kit checklist

- A brush for cleaning the cage.
- Rubber gloves.
- A scoop or spatula for scooping out droppings.
- A bottle-brush for cleaning out the water bottle.
- A safe pet disinfectant cleaner from a pet store.
- A bucket for water.

Weekly cleaning

Once a week, you need to clean out the cage or hutch completely. First, put the rabbit somewhere safe, such as in a **run**. Then remove all bedding from the hutch. Scrub the hutch with warm soapy water or water mixed with a mild pet **disinfectant**. Make sure you clean the whole cage, especially in the corners. Then rinse the cage with clean water. Wait until it is completely dry before you put in clean bedding and flooring materials.

You should clean a rabbit cage or hutch once a week. Always wear gloves when you do this, and wash your hands when you have finished.

Make sure you have enough clean bedding before you start.

Top tip

Rabbits often use the same corner of the cage as their toilet area. When you replace sawdust or wood shavings after cleaning, put more in this spot to help absorb **urine** and droppings.

29

Grooming

Rabbits are clean animals and regularly **groom** themselves. They use their teeth and tongue to clean their fur. Brushing your rabbit helps her to stay clean and healthy, and most rabbits enjoy it.

Sit your rabbit on some newspaper or an old towel. Use a soft bristle brush or a comb and start at the head and neck, and brush in the direction in which the fur grows. Brush your rabbit all over, including her stomach, armpits, and around and under her tail, but be gentle.

Rabbits clean their whole body, including their long ears.

Moulting

Rabbits **moult** (lose) some of their fur once or twice a year. New fur grows in its place. It is important to groom rabbits more often at these times to prevent **fur balls**. Fur balls can be dangerous because they can get stuck in a rabbit's throat.

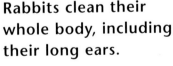

Most rabbits enjoy being groomed.

Going away

Your rabbit will be fine if you go away for the night, as long as you leave water, hay, and food in her hutch. When you go away for longer than one night, you must get someone else to look after her. If you have to move your rabbit, get a pet-carrying basket or cage to take her to her holiday home. Make a list of all the things she will need, such as food and toys. Write down her playing and cleaning routines, and pass this list to the person who will be looking after her.

Baskets for carrying rabbits are usually made of plastic or wicker. You can get temporary baskets made of tough cardboard, too.

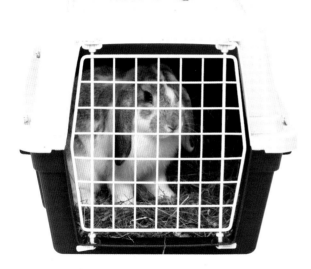

Check up!

When you groom your rabbit, check to see that she is healthy. Here are some things to look out for. See pages 38–41 for advice on looking after your rabbit's health.

- Does she come to the front of the cage to meet you? Is she moving differently? Rabbits that stay huddled up in a corner may be feeling sick.
- Is she scratching more than usual? If so, she may have fleas.
- Check the hair under the tail, especially in long-haired rabbits. If this area is dirty in summer, flies may lay their eggs here. This can cause a serious disease called flystrike. If you see flies or eggs here, take your rabbit straight to a vet.
- When grooming, check for fleas and mites. These are tiny **parasites** that can live on your rabbit's skin.

andling your rabbit

Many rabbits become tame and happy to be handled (picked up) after some careful, patient training. However, some rabbits may never enjoy being handled. If your rabbit does not like being held, do not be disappointed. Just find other ways of enjoying his company.

First steps

Before handling your rabbit, let him get to know you. Let him out of his cage somewhere quiet and safe. Lie on the floor and let him come to you. Be patient and eventually he will come over to sniff you. Do not grab him. Let him hop around you and over you as he gets to know your smell.

When your rabbit feels safe with you, try stroking him between the ears. Then you can stroke his back, let him lie with you, and eventually start to play together. If you give him time to get to know you, he will think of you as a friend.

Offer your rabbit a treat from your hand, such as a piece of apple or carrot, while he is getting to know you.

 Take care!

Rabbit bones break easily if they fall. If your rabbit tries to get away from you, he may bite or scratch you. So, if your rabbit struggles when you hold him, hug him firmly but gently to your chest to stop him clawing you. Kneel and put him down so he is facing you, back legs first. Rabbits are less likely to jump if they cannot see where they are going.

Picking rabbits up

Pick a rabbit up from the front, not from behind, because he may kick out in surprise. Wear gloves until you get used to doing this, in case your rabbit scratches. With one hand, hold him gently by the scruff (back) of his neck. Use your other arm to support his back end as you lift him up. Or you can hold one hand under the front and the other under the back end of his body. When you pick your rabbit up, hold him against your chest or shoulder, or sit with him on your lap so he feels safe.

This is a safe way to pick up a rabbit.

You can lift a rabbit like this. Most of the rabbit's weight should be on the lower hand. Always lift a rabbit carefully and gently.

Top tips
- Never lift your rabbit up just by the scruff of the neck, or by his ears, as this can hurt him badly.
- Do not lift him too high. If he wriggles and falls, he may injure himself.

33

Reward good behaviour

You may be able to train some rabbits to stop unwanted behaviour such as chewing furniture or leaving droppings out of the **litter tray**. When the rabbit does these things, just say "no" firmly, and point your finger at the rabbit. If she stops, reward your rabbit by stroking her or giving her a food treat.

It is natural for rabbits to chew and dig. They can be quite destructive. If you cannot get your rabbit to play by the rules, you will have to rabbit-proof your home. That way, you and your rabbit can enjoy her playtime without you worrying.

Top tip

Rabbits cannot be expected to use their litter tray all the time. When they are young, let them play out for a short time before feeding them. They usually get better as they get older, but even then they might leave droppings where they shouldn't.

Running away

If your rabbit keeps running away when it is time to go back into her hutch, or escapes and gets stuck behind a piece of furniture, stay calm. If you shout, you will frighten her. First, try tempting her closer with food. Do not try to grab her suddenly or she will run away again. Let the rabbit eat. Talk gently as she eats to keep her calm. Then gently and calmly pick her up and put her back in her hutch.

When training your rabbit, reward her with lots of stroking and petting.

Never shout at or punish your rabbit, or she will become frightened of you. Just say "no" firmly and help to keep her out of trouble.

Why does my rabbit bite me?

- Some rabbits scratch or bite because they do not want to be held.
- Some rabbits bite if you offer them your hand to sniff. This is because rabbits cannot see just in front of their nose. They may get scared when they see movement and think you are an attacker.

Be patient if your rabbit will not go back into her cage. Try using food to lure stubborn rabbits back to their cage.

Understanding your rabbit

It is important to know why your rabbit behaves as he does, so you understand what he wants and needs. That way you will know when he is fed up and does not want to be handled anymore, or when he is happy and wants a cuddle.

When your rabbit is happy and content he will lie stretched out on the floor, often with both eyes closed. Sometimes he will make a chattering sound with his teeth, or hum or purr when he is happy. When your rabbit is scared, he will lie still, close to the ground, with his ears back and eyes open. When your rabbit is angry, he may stomp his back feet on the ground and make a noise that sounds a bit like "oont"!

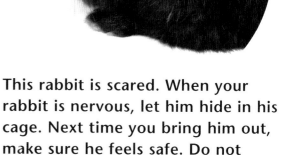

Scent marking

When your rabbit rubs his chin against you or objects, it does not mean he is itchy or hurt. He is just marking the things with his scent (which we cannot smell), so he feels at home around them.

This rabbit is scared. When your rabbit is nervous, let him hide in his cage. Next time you bring him out, make sure he feels safe. Do not grab him – let him come to you.

This rabbit is scent-marking the furniture in his home.

Playtime

Set aside some time every day to play with your rabbits. Play helps your rabbits think of you as a friend and stops them from getting bored. Some pet shops sell rabbit toys, or you can make your own.

You could build a maze using pipes and cardboard boxes for your rabbits to explore. You can stuff hay into a cardboard box, tube, or a paper bag for your rabbits to play with. Good chew toys that help keep rabbits' teeth short are pine cones, egg cartons, apple twigs, and old wooden spoons. Some rabbits like to hide in paper bags or make nests in old towels. Many rabbits like hard plastic toys, such as clean laundry detergent balls that they can move and roll about.

Top tip

Check plastic toys regularly and replace them if they are damaged. Small bits of plastic can be dangerous if your rabbit swallows them.

Rabbits like to be given new toys or objects to play with.

Rabbit walking

Some people take their rabbits for a slow walk around the garden on a special harness and lead. Never pull a rabbit on a lead or put a **harness** on if he does not like it, and do not use it for long.

Health matters

Most rabbits are healthy animals if they are looked after properly. You should keep an eye on your rabbit for any signs that she is unwell. Rabbits can get seriously ill very quickly. If you think your rabbit might be ill, take her to the vet immediately. Here are some things to ask your vet about.

Vaccinations are quick and painless.

Vaccinations

Young rabbits need **vaccinations**. These are **injections** that protect them against diseases. Ask your vet about what types of vaccination your rabbits need and how often they need booster injections to keep them safe.

Claws have to be trimmed carefully so the skin around them is not damaged.

Teeth and claws

Check your rabbit's teeth and claws regularly to see that they do not become overgrown. Overgrown claws are easily torn when caught in fabric or wire mesh.

Overgrown teeth can cause mouth **sores** and eventually prevent your rabbit from eating. Sores that develop on overgrown back teeth can swell up. They will press on the back of a rabbit's eyes and damage them. In severe cases this can even cause blindness. If your rabbit's teeth or claws grow too long, take her to the vet to have them cut or clipped.

Fleas, lice, and mites

If you see your rabbit constantly scratching herself, she may have fleas, lice, or mites. These tiny insects are **parasites**. Check with the vet if you are not sure what is causing the itching, and treat the problem with special powders or sprays from the vet or pet shop.

Top tip

Fleas **reproduce** by laying eggs in the rabbit's flooring or bedding. If your rabbit has fleas, you need to get rid of all the hay, newspaper, wood shavings, and sawdust. Clean the cage carefully to prevent your rabbit getting more fleas.

You can clean a small wound yourself. Make sure you ask an adult to help you.

Wounds

When rabbits live together, they may fight or accidentally hurt each other. Bathe wounds in a mild **antiseptic** lotion. If wounds are bad or they do not heal, take your rabbit to a vet. If your rabbits continue to fight, put them in separate cages.

39

Eyes

If your rabbit has red, sore, or weeping eyes, he may have an **infection**. Ask an adult to bathe the eyes with cotton wool and cool, boiled water. If the eyes do not get better, go to the vet. Eye problems are often caused by dust or draughts, so buy dust-free hay and keep the cage out of draughts.

Ears

The skin in a rabbit's ears should be pink and cool, not red or hot. The ears should look clean. If your rabbit keeps scratching his ears, shakes or holds his head oddly, loses his balance, or if his ears look dirty inside, he may have ear canker. Tiny insects called ear mites cause this uncomfortable condition. You should ask your vet how to treat it.

You could wrap a towel around your rabbit to stop him from struggling when you give him eyedrops.

Constipation and diarrhoea

Constipation and **diarrhoea** are problems caused by your rabbit eating too much, or by not eating enough of the right food. Constipation is when your rabbit produces very hard droppings that are difficult to pass. Giving your rabbit more green leafy vegetables to eat usually cures constipation.

Diarrhoea is when droppings are very runny. You can usually cure this by feeding your rabbit only hay and water and no green vegetables for 24 hours. If diarrhoea or constipation goes on for more than a couple of days, take your rabbit to a vet.

Eating extra green foods can cure a rabbit's constipation.

Snuffles

If your rabbit sneezes a lot and gets a runny nose, he could have a disease called "snuffles". Snuffles can turn into **pneumonia**, which can kill rabbits. Take your rabbit to a vet right away. Snuffles is also very **infectious**. To stop other rabbits from catching it, put the sick rabbit into a separate cage until he gets better.

Top tip

Check the bowl and bottle to see if your rabbit is eating his food and drinking enough water. If he is leaving more than usual, he may be ill.

Overheating

Rabbits get overheated easily, so keep them in shade on hot days. If they pant, dribble, and go a bit limp, they may be overheated. Spray or bathe them in cool water to cool them down. Take your rabbit to a vet if this does not help.

Spraying an overheated rabbit helps him to cool down.

Getting older

As rabbits get older, they slow down. They play less, and rest and sleep more often. They may need more help to keep themselves clean because they cannot stretch to **groom** themselves. They may also get ill more often, so regular check-ups with a vet are a good idea.

As rabbits get old, they may sleep more and be less playful than they were.

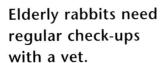

Elderly rabbits need regular check-ups with a vet.

Changes

Most rabbits get slower as they get older. Some get **arthritis**, a condition that makes it hard for them to run or climb. They will need less food because they are less active. If you give the same amount of food, they may get too fat and this can lead to health problems. Some older rabbits also become unable to **digest** dried rabbit food mixes. They may be healthier if they eat a diet of hay, some vegetables, and less or no dried food.

A peaceful end

Many rabbits die peacefully in their sleep when their body is too old or tired to work anymore. Some rabbits may get very ill. If your rabbit finds it difficult to feed, move around, or if she is in pain and suffering from a long-term illness, your vet may decide that the best option is to put her to sleep. This means that the vet will give your rabbit a special **injection** or gas to stop her breathing. This is a painless, gentle way to stop an animal from suffering.

When a pet dies

It is very hard to lose a pet. When your rabbit dies, you may feel angry, lonely, confused, or sad. This is normal. Try to remember that it is no-one's fault. Talking to your family and friends about how you feel may help. They will probably understand just how you feel.

Saying goodbye

Some people bury their pets in their garden. Doing this gives them a chance to say goodbye and think about the happy times they had with their pet.

You could plant flowers or make a sign to mark the spot where you bury your pet rabbit.

Keeping a record

Your rabbit should be with you for many years. It is a great idea to keep a record of your time together. Start when your rabbit is young and first comes home. Try to add to your record throughout your rabbit's life.

You might like to include pictures of any pet shows your rabbit enters or wins. You could include any ribbons or certificates that he wins.

Top tip

Keep a record of your rabbit's **vaccinations** so you can check they are up-to-date.

You could collect photos like this one. It shows you are your rabbit's favourite person!

Diaries and scrapbooks

The best way to keep a rabbit record is to make a diary or scrapbook. You can write or stick in almost anything you like. Include photos of special times, such as the first time you brought your rabbit home. Write down your rabbit's likes, dislikes, and favourite people. You could write down the dates when he explored your room for the first time, or learned to use a **litter tray**. And you could keep a record of what his favourite food is.

Rabbit care

You could also include general information about rabbits and stick in articles about how to care for pet rabbits properly. You could include photos out of magazines, or print out pictures of other rabbit **breeds** from the Internet.

Top tip

Include facts about your rabbit's routine, and the things he likes and does not like, in your diary. Then the book becomes a useful guide for the people who look after your rabbit when you go away on holiday.

It is a good idea to add some dates to your photos. This also makes it more interesting for other people to look at.

Glossary

anaesthetic   medicine to make an animal sleep during an operation

animal shelter   place where pets that have been abandoned or badly treated are cared for until they find a new home

antiseptic   something that keeps a wound free from germs

arthritis   condition in which an animal's joints become sore and swollen

breeder   someone who raises a particular type of animal. A rabbit breeder keeps rabbits so he or she can sell their babies.

breeds   different types of rabbit, for example, Angora and Agouti

burrow   hole in the ground

constipation   problem caused when an animal's droppings (poo) are very hard, making it difficult for it to go to the toilet

diarrhoea   runny droppings

digest   when animals take goodness from food as it passes through their body

digestive system   parts of the body that digest food

disinfectant   spray or liquid that kills germs

domesticate   to tame an animal so that it can live with people

electrocuted   when an animal is killed because electricity flows through it

fibre   part of the food animals eat. Fibre keeps their digestive systems healthy.

fur balls   tangled lumps of old hair that get caught in an animal's throat

grain   seed of a cereal plant such as wheat or corn

groom   to clean an animal's fur. Many animals groom themselves.

hutch   rabbit home

infection   disease in a part of your body that is caused by bacteria or a virus

infectious   when a disease is easily passed on to other animals

injection   when a needle is used to put medicine into an animal's body

litter   a number of baby animals born together

litter tray   tray where rabbits can leave their droppings and urine

mammal   animal that gives birth to live babies and feeds them with milk from its own body

moult   when an animal's fur drops out to be replaced by a new coat

neutered   when part of a male animal's sexual organs are removed so that he cannot have babies

nutrients   parts of food that an animal's body needs to grow and keep healthy

parasite   animal that lives and feeds on another animal's body

pest   animal that causes problems for people

pneumonia   illness where the lungs become infected and full of pus

reproduce   when animals produce young

rescue home   place where abandoned pets are cared for until they find a new home

RSPCA   agency that works to prevent cruelty to animals

run   enclosure that rabbits can run and exercise in, either outdoors or indoors

sores   red, painful spots on the skin

spayed   when part of a female animal's sexual organs are removed so that she cannot have babies

urine   wee, a waste liquid that is released by an animal's body

vaccination   injection that protects an animal against a disease

warm-blooded   describes an animal that can warm up or cool down to adapt to its surroundings

Further reading

Care for Your Rabbit (RSPCA Pet Guides series), (Collins, 2004)

Rabbit (Looking After Your Pet series), Clare Hibbert (Hodder Books, 2004)

Small Pet Care: How to Look After Your Rabbit, Guinea Pig, or Hamster, Annabel Blackledge (Dorling Kindersley, 2005)

The Wild Side of Pet Rabbits, Jo Waters (Raintree, 2005)

Useful addresses

Most countries have organizations and societies that work to protect animals from cruelty, and to help people learn how to care for the pets they live with properly.

UK
Royal Society for the Prevention
   of Cruelty to Animals (RSPCA)
Wilberforce Way
Southwater
Horsham
West Sussex
RH13 9RS
Tel: 0870 33 35 999
Fax: 0870 75 30 284

Australia
RSPCA Australia Inc.
PO Box 265
Deakin West ACT 2600
Australia
Tel.: 02 6282 8300
Fax: 02 6282 8311

Internet

There are hundreds of pet websites on the Internet. They give information about caring for your pet and advice on the kinds of equipment that you might need. These sites have information aimed at young people.

You can print advice sheets about rabbit care from the BBC website:
www.bbc.co.uk/cbbc/wild/pets/rabbit.shtml

The UK RSPCA website www.rspca.org.uk has a lot of information about rabbit care. Search under "Animals" or "Animal care".

Disclaimer
All the Internet addresses (URLs) given in this book were valid at the time of going to press. However, due to the dynamic nature of the Internet, some addresses may have changed, or sites may have changed or ceased to exist since publication. While the author and Publishers regret any inconvenience this may cause readers, no responsibility for any such changes can be accepted by either the author or the Publishers.

Index

Titles in the *Keeping Pets* series include:

Hardback   0 431 12424 8

Hardback   0 431 12425 6

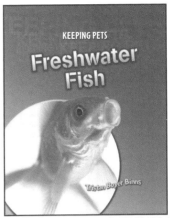

Hardback   0 431 12426 4

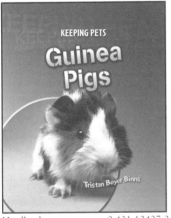

Hardback   0 431 12427 2

Hardback   0 431 12428 0

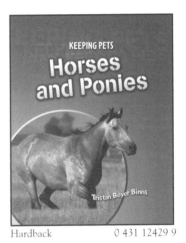

Hardback   0 431 12429 9

Hardback   0 431 12448 5

Hardback   0 431 12449 3

Find out about other titles from Heinemann Library on our website www.heinemann.co.uk/library